Go West

THE RISK & THE REWARD

Published by Range Conservation Foundation & RANGE magazine

C.J. Hadley, publisher/editor

Rod Miller, senior writer

Publisher/Editor: C.J. Hadley
Concept & Design: John Bardwell
Senior Writer: Rod Miller
Staff: Ann Galli, Joani Haws, Joyce Smith, Denyse Pellettieri White

Library of Congress Cataloging-in-Publication Data
Hadley, C.J.
Go West
Caroline Joy Hadley
ISBN 9780964745605
LCCN 2012912696

Published by the Range Conservation Foundation and RANGE magazine, Carson City, Nevada, with assistance from the Nevada Rangeland Resources

$32 U.S.A.
Printed in China

PHOTO: Sierra Nevada range, looking at 14,497-foot Mount Whitney, the highest summit in the contiguous United States. This is late afternoon in Death Valley and the view is toward the Cottonwood Mountains from Black Mountains.
© Larry Angier

> "Eastward I go only by force;
> But westward I go free."
>
> HENRY DAVID THOREAU, 1851

Go West

The Risk

Ready yourself for hunger. Outfit yourself for fatigue. Pack for accidents. Expect endless plains, insurmountable mountains, dreadful deserts.

Prepare to die.

Guidebooks and promoters of Manifest Destiny urging folks to "Go West" neglected to include that advice.

But would it have mattered? Most who set out for The West back then may well have snugged up cinches, strapped on harnesses, yoked up teams and set out anyway. For, regardless of risk, the lure—and the lore—was irresistible for many.

Hundreds of thousands took to the trails seeking land, independence, freedom, riches, and any number of other rewards for answering the call to "Go West."

The Reward

Some sought a Promised Land. Others Zion. Still others the Garden of Eden. And, some, streets paved with gold.

No matter what drove their hunger, their want, their need, most who followed the admonition to "Go West" were rewarded for the effort. Even those who did not find what they were looking for still found themselves blessed in a land like no other. Vast miles of incomparable rangeland. Unmatched mountain splendor reaching into boundless blue skies. Sunshine and snow. Priceless water. And, most of all, neighbors beyond value.

Together, those neighbors built a way of life that melds a diversity of cultures, a love for the land, an affection for freedom, and a unique blend of cooperation and self-reliance.

They built, in other words, "The West."

Westward, Ever Westward

By Rod Miller

G o West, young man, go West." Newspaperman Horace
Greeley is credited with saying this back in the 1830s...or
1850s...or 1860s. Or maybe he said, "Go West, young man, and
grow up with the country." Then again, it might have been, "If
any young man is about to commence the world, we say to him,
publicly and privately, Go to the West."

But no matter what Greeley said, when he said it, or even if
he said it at all, the fact is...the idea, the inspiration, the aspiration captured in those few words describes, perhaps better than
any other, the course of American history.

Others have voiced the same notion. In his 1851 essay "Walk-
ing," philosopher Henry David Thoreau wrote, "Eastward I go
only by force; but westward I go free." Henry Wells, the express-
man who teamed up with William G. Fargo to help open the
West, said it this way, "Westward, ever westward."

Even before America existed, William Shakespeare foreshad-
owed the same idea. In his 1602 play, "Twelfth Night," Olivia tells
Viola, "There lies your way, due-west." Viola's immortal response
is, "Then westward-ho."

Within a decade of Shakespeare's foretelling, English settlers
traveled west and colonized Virginia. Shortly afterward, the
British and other Europeans came ashore farther north in what
would become New England. They weren't the first, mind you.
The French and the Spanish had been in Florida since at least the
1560s, but they seemed content to stay put. Those farther north,

*Rocky Mountain thunderstorm in northern
San Luis Valley, Colorado. © Larry Angier*

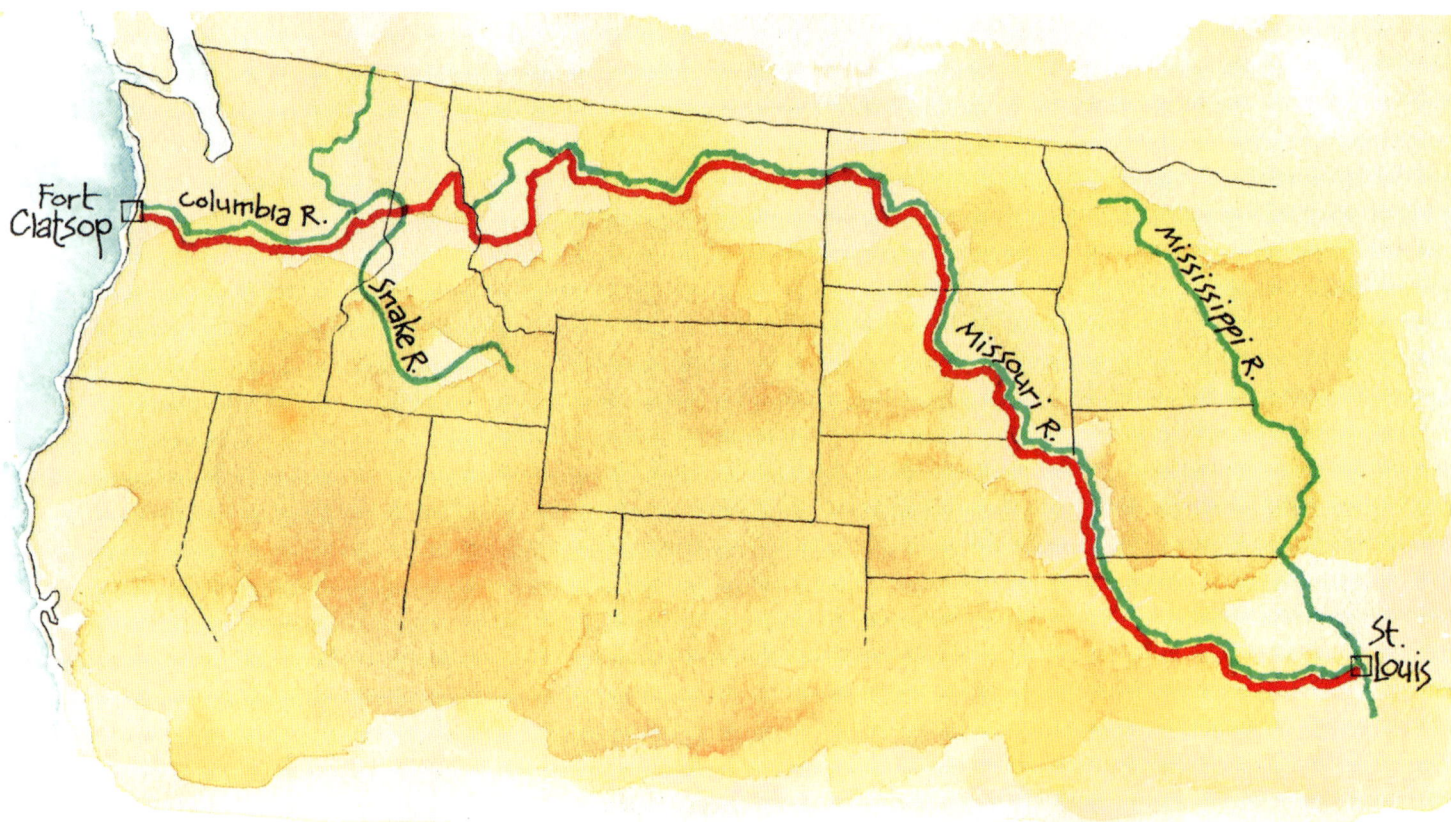

Illustration © John Bardwell

Shortly after President Thomas Jefferson purchased Louisiana from the French in 1803, he sent military officers Meriwether Lewis and William Clark to see what he'd bought. Leading the Corps of Discovery, Lewis and Clark set out in 1804 and followed the Missouri River to its headwaters at the Continental Divide, the western border of the newly acquired territory. But they didn't stop there, crossing the divide in search of a route to Oregon and to establish a claim to that country. After a winter on the shores of the Pacific Ocean, the expedition returned to the States in 1806, carrying with them scientific observations and samples of the plants and wildlife and weather they encountered; maps of rivers and mountains, trails and trade routes; and detailed accounts of Indian nations encountered along the way. The knowledge gained by Lewis and Clark was instrumental in opening the West to trappers and traders, explorers and settlers.

on the other hand, almost immediately started nosing their way westward. In Virginia and in the Carolinas, settlements crept across the Tidewater region, up the Piedmont, and into the Appalachians. Farther north still, the Ohio River and Cumberland Gap opened the way West, led by legendary explorers like Daniel Boone.

The British, the French, and the Spanish had already become largely irrelevant with the birth of the United States of America in 1776, and citizens of the new confederation grew even more inclined toward the West. With President Thomas Jefferson's 1803 Louisiana Purchase, the infant nation laid claim to mostly unknown lands from the Mississippi River to the Continental Divide. But Jefferson's vision did not stop at the summits of the Rocky Mountains—in 1804, he sent Lewis and Clark and the Corps of Discovery to explore the new territory and go beyond to the Pacific Ocean. Zebulon Pike set out in 1806 on an expedition to map the southern regions of the Louisiana Purchase and made his way to what is now Colorado. He eventually landed in a prison in Chihuahua for encroaching into Spanish territory.

Before either expedition returned, others with different interests followed their footsteps into the West. Traders, trappers, and mountain men moved onto the plains and into the high country in pursuit of fur—and adventure. Some came and went and left nothing behind. Others are known by their names stamped on the map of the West: John Colter, Joe Walker, Jedediah Smith, Jim Bridger, Kit Carson, William Ashley, Davey Jackson, Bill Sublette, Etienne Provost, Peter Ogden, Benjamin Bonneville. The knowledge they gained of travel routes and trails, landscapes and landmarks, rivers and streams, mountain ranges and valleys would prove invaluable as many of them later guided explorers and settlers into the wide-open spaces of the West.

Hot on their heels were military and scientific expeditions sent to fill in the vast, empty spaces on these maps drawn by Lewis and Clark and Pike and to take stock of the country's resources. John Charles Fremont is most likely the best known of the bunch, thanks to both effective public relations and the guidance of Kit Carson. Other military expeditions were led by Stephen H. Long, Gouverneur Warren, William F. Raynolds, William Emory, Joseph Nicollet, Charles Wilkes, and others who meandered through and mapped the West.

One military man, Randolph B. Marcy, aided the westward migration with the government-sponsored publication of "The Prairie Traveler: A Handbook for Overland Expeditions, with Maps, Illustrations, and Itineraries of the Principal Routes Between the Mississippi and the Pacific." It was a helpful guide, offering advice on everything from laying in supplies to packing a wagon to caring for draft animals. And most emigrants needed the advice, venturing into a country the likes of which they could not even imagine.

Folklore has it that back in those days a squirrel could travel the treetops from the East Coast to the Mississippi River and never touch the ground. Beyond the Mississippi, for squirrels and travelers alike, things were different. Timber thinned out until it eventually disappeared. In the Great Plains, climbing to the High Plains, grass rolled on forever—a naked landscape to those com-

Legendary fur trapper turned guide and trader, Jim Bridger used his vast knowledge of the West to aid many an emigrant. His Fort Bridger, in today's southwestern Wyoming, was one of few stops on the Oregon/California/Mormon Trail where travelers could buy supplies, trade livestock, and get the latest travel advice and information.

Military explorer John C. Fremont traveled widely across the unknown West, and the maps and reports from his 1842 and 1843 expeditions were instrumental in informing westbound emigrants. His knowledge stretched from the Platte River to the Snake, from the Great Salt Lake to Sacramento and beyond.

Kit Carson broke and followed trails all over the West as a mountain man, scout, Indian fighter, and military guide. Much of Fremont's success resulted from Carson's ability as a frontiersman. His name appears on cities, mountains, valleys, rivers, passes, roads, trails, forts, and national forests throughout the West.

The Columbia River rises in the Rocky Mountains of British Columbia, Canada, and flows northwest and then south into the state of Washington. At 1,243 miles long, its drainage basin is roughly the size of France. This is the Columbia Plateau. © Tom Stack/Tom Stack & Associates

The Columbia River Gorge is a canyon of the Columbia River in the Pacific Northwest. Up to 4,000 feet deep, the canyon stretches for more than 80 miles as the river winds westward through the Cascade Range forming the boundary between the states of Washington and Oregon. It is the only navigable route through the Cascades and the only water connection between the Columbia River Plateau and the Pacific Ocean. © Paul Marcellini/Tom Stack & Associates

ing from the forested East.

When military explorer and engineer Stephen H. Long visited the plains, his 1820 report dubbed the region "the great American desert." He wrote, "In regard to this extensive section of the country, I do not hesitate in giving the opinion that it is almost wholly unfit for cultivation, and, of course, uninhabitable by a people depending upon agriculture for their subsistence." In the 1880s, when Theodore Roosevelt—who would later become president of the United States—took up ranching in the Dakota Territory, the emptiness of the land affected him. He said, "Nowhere, not at sea, does a man feel more lonely than when riding over the far-reaching, seemingly never-ending plains."

Many who headed West saw the plains as something to pass over. And once they cleared that obstacle, they were faced with range after range of the Rocky Mountains—the Wind River, the Wasatch, the Portneuf, the Goose Creeks, and more—then the Sierra Nevada, the Cascades. The arid valleys and deserts in between were sometimes seen as nothing more than more unpleasant obstacles. If place names are any indication, the West was downright evil: Devils Slide, Devils Gate, Devils Canyon, Devils Tower, Hells Half Acre, Hells Backbone, Hells Bend, Hells

Canyon. All in all, most westbound travelers were happy to put what we now call "the West" behind them and push on to less hostile and more hospitable environs in California and the Oregon Territory.

Which brings up a question: What, exactly, is the West?

Defining the West is an arguable proposition, but many—maybe most—would agree that it comprises the region west of the 100th meridian and east of the Sierra Nevada and Cascade mountain ranges. The meridian roughly halves the Dakotas near the Missouri River, cleanly divides Nebraska, slices off a third of Kansas, and separates Texas from the panhandle west. It's a line west of which rainfall is too scarce to grow crops. Beyond the Sierra and Cascades, the climate and terrain change markedly.

So in that sense at least, the West is clearly defined. It's a vast and varied region, both rich and poor—poor in water, but, in places, rich in minerals, in rangeland, in timber, in beauty. And that richness eventually encouraged the westbound to linger, explore, exploit, even settle the plains, mountains, and valleys of what we now consider the West.

Graduates of the fur trade set up shop to supply passing emigrants. Fort Laramie, Fort Bridger, Fort Hall, and Fort Boise

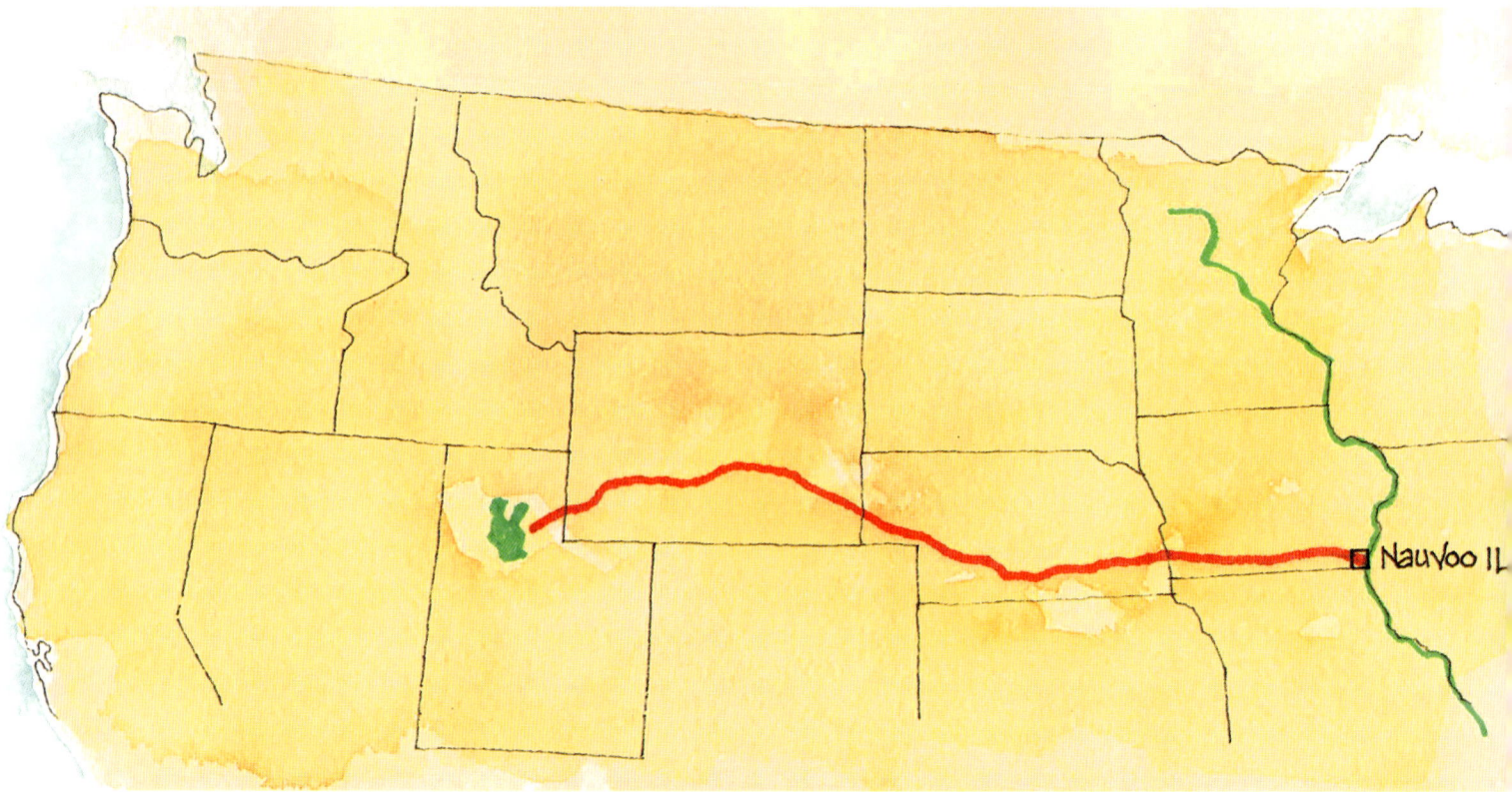

Unable to get along with their neighbors wherever they settled, Mormons—members of the Church of Jesus Christ of Latter-day Saints—were hounded out of New York, Ohio, Missouri, and Illinois. Brigham Young, the sect's second leader, opted to abandon the United States and decamped to Mexico, settling on the shores of the Great Salt Lake. The Mexican War trumped Mormon intentions of an independent nation, making them, once again, Americans. In spite of political and religious disagreements, the organized exodus of tens of thousands of Mormons was instrumental in the settlement of the West. The Mormon Trail is 1,300 miles long. Illustration © John Bardwell

> "Looked starvation in the face. I have seen men on passing an animal that has starved to death on the plains stop and cut out a steak, roast and eat it and call it delicious."
>
> CLARK THOMPSON, EMIGRANT, 1850

The Snake is a major river of the greater Pacific Northwest. At 1,078 miles long, it is the largest tributary of the Columbia, the largest North American river that empties into the Pacific Ocean. Rising in western Wyoming, the river flows through the Snake River Plain (above), then rugged Hells Canyon and the rolling Palouse Hills to reach its mouth, and the confluence of the Yakima, Snake and Columbia rivers in the semiarid regions of southeastern Washington. Snake River Plain is a vast depression that stretches across southern Idaho in an arc about 60 miles wide and nearly 400 miles long. The area has been subject to volcanism for the last sixteen million years, resulting in the accumulation of thousands of feet of ash and rhyolite. For the last two million years, the area has been torn by rift zones due to stretching of the continental crust. Basalt flows have poured from these rifts, filling the basin and creating this flat, stark landscape. The peak on the horizon is Big Southern Butte, a complex of rhyolite domes formed about 300,000 years ago. View is looking southeast from Craters of the Moon National Monument in Butte County, Idaho. © Ron Wolf/Tom Stack & Associates

Reality on the pioneer trails was not as pleasant and easy as this woodcut suggests.

Bad advice led to one of the most storied tragedies of the westward migration. The story of the Donner Party started off well enough, when a wagon train set off from Missouri in 1846 along the established trails. But near Fort Bridger the train split apart, with one faction led by George Donner and James Reed opting to follow a new, shorter trail promoted by Lansford Hastings, which would take them over the Wasatch Mountains and across the Great Salt Lake Desert to meet the Humboldt River and rejoin the California Trail. Breaking trail through the mountains, bogging down in desert mud, and the loss of draft animals slowed the eighty-seven-member Donner-Reed party, and early winter storms caught them unaware and unprepared high in the Sierra Nevada near Truckee Lake. Many died of cold and starvation; others survived by dining on the corpses of their fallen comrades. When finally rescued, only forty-eight survived to settle in California.

Carson Pass in the Sierra Nevada (now Eldorado National Forest) sits at 8,574 feet and connects Sacramento Valley, California, to Carson Valley, Nevada. © Larry Angier

"A country of starvation."

JOSEPH REDDEFORD WALKER, EXPLORER,
EXPLAINING THE GREAT BASIN IN 1826

were important and much anticipated way stations along the wagon roads where travelers could rest up and resupply.

The first and most significant settlers were the Mormons. These driven members of the Church of Jesus Christ of Latter-day Saints established Great Salt Lake City on the shores of its namesake in 1847 and soon rooted settlements all along the eastern rim of the Great Basin. They sent tentacles far to the south to establish Las Vegas and San Bernardino, north to the Salmon River to set up Fort Limhi, and west to the opposite rim of the Great Basin to an outpost at Mormon Station on the lee side of the Sierra where Genoa, Nevada, now stands.

But the Salt Lake Valley is where the Mormons started in the West, and where they stayed, hoping they had at last found their Promised Land, their Zion. Upon entering the valley in July 1847 after a thousand-mile journey across plains and mountains, Orson Pratt, one of Mormon leader Brigham Young's apostles, recorded, "We could not refrain from a shout of joy, which almost involuntarily escaped from our lips the moment this grand and lovely scenery was within our view." The bliss, however, was not universal. Harriet, Young's sister-in-law, said, "Weak and weary as I am, I would rather go a thousand miles farther than remain in such a forsaken place as this." Despite her misgivings, where the Mormons found water, they found possibilities in the forsaken place.

But they were not the first to see potential in the valleys that lined the Wasatch range. In 1776, Spanish Padres Dominguez and Escalante, seeking a shortcut from Santa Fe to Monterey, followed the Spanish Fork River out of the Wasatch Mountains and found themselves in Utah Valley, just over the ridge from where the Mormons eventually settled some forty miles to the north. "Over and above these finest of advantages," Escalante recorded in the expedition's journal, "it has plenty of firewood and timber in the adjacent sierra which surrounds it—many sheltered spots, waters, and pasturages, for raising cattle and sheep and horses."

Still, despite the permanence of the Mormons in the Mountain West, most emigrants passed through the country. Oregon-bound settlers passed to the north; some on the way to California stopped in Salt Lake City to replenish supplies and trade for fresh horses and oxen. But the Mormons were as short on essentials as the travelers were. They may well have starved out if not for the discovery of gold (by Mormons, as it happens) in California. For years, westbound gold seekers poured into the valley by the thousands, bringing with them much-needed cash to equip themselves for the remainder of the trek.

The forty-niners were mostly men intending to strike it rich and return home. Few accomplished the first, but many managed the second. It seemed there was always the lure of another rich strike somewhere when the gold or silver ran out. Opportunists chased ore from one end of the West to the other, as boomtowns sprouted seemingly overnight. Some towns withered just as quickly; other towns struggled stubbornly to save themselves, if only as shadows of their former glory.

There were Belleville and Bodie in California; Bannack and Butte in Montana; Deadwood and Lead in the Dakotas; Coeur d'Alene and Idaho City in Idaho; Cherry Creek and Creede in Colorado; South Pass City and Encampment in Wyoming; Park City and Bingham Canyon in Utah; Tombstone and Bisbee in Arizona; and Goldfield and, greatest of all, the Comstock Lode in Nevada. There were more...many more. Prospectors and miners were by nature fiddle-footed, ever ready to pull up stakes and light out for the next big chance.

So while mining did little to foster permanent settlement, it did result in widespread familiarity of the vast territories out West, and helped create a romanticized version of the country through purple prose in periodicals and dime novels.

Meanwhile, back in Washington, D.C., manifest destiny—the notion that it was inevitable, and only right, that the United States would occupy the continent from sea to shining sea—was in full swing.

Texans received unofficial encouragement and assistance in their separation from Mexico in 1836, and the short-lived Republic joined the American nation in 1845.

The annexation of Texas was one of many explanations for an opportunistic war against Mexico in 1846 that ended with the Treaty of Guadalupe Hidalgo in 1848. Its terms ceded much of Mexico to the victor: Alta California in its entirety; all of what would eventually become Arizona, slices of New Mexico and Colorado; and the Mormon kingdom of Deseret, which the nation would divide into the present states of Utah and Nevada and a corner of Wyoming.

After years of joint occupation with England and much quibbling, the Oregon Territory was organized in 1848, adding the

Meteor over Great Salt Lake, Utah.
The photographer's "NightScapes" are made with evening time exposures and often include star constellations and the Milky Way, without motion blurring.
© Royce Bair, www.NightScapePhotos.com

Pacific Northwest, where Lewis and Clark had trod all those years earlier, to the nation. Eventually, the states of Washington, Oregon, Idaho, and parts of Wyoming and Montana resulted.

But statehood and self-determination were slow to come to much of the West, owing to a weak federal government's struggles with the states over where and when slavery would be allowed. It took the Civil War to eventually sort it all out, and, in the case of Utah, a long struggle over loyalty and the Mormons' practice of allowing a man to have multiple wives. New Mexico and Arizona came late to the party, admitted to the Union in 1912, finally completing a coast-to-coast patchwork of United States.

All that aside, by 1848, New York journalist John L. Sullivan's 1845 claim that it was the nation's "manifest destiny to overspread and to possess the whole of the continent which Providence has given us for the development of the great experiment of liberty and federated self-government entrusted to us" was, for all practical purposes, fulfilled.

Americans viewed all this expansion as occurring, essentially, in empty and unoccupied land. Little thought was given to its native inhabitants other than getting them out of the way as efficiently as possible. Wars played a role, as did the spread of disease and the extermination of buffalo and other wildlife, occupation of prime land, control of water, and the eradication of other essentials to the Indian way of life.

This, of course, was not exclusive to expansion of the West; it had been underway since the first Europeans set foot in the "New World" in the fifteenth century. As acclaimed Indian fighter General Nelson Miles put it, "Step by step a powerful and enterprising race has driven them back from the Atlantic to the West until at last there is scarcely a spot of ground upon which the Indians have any certainty of maintaining a permanent abode."

So, now that the United States had fulfilled its destiny to own the West, the question was what to do with it. Aside from a significant population hugging the West Coast, clusters of Mormons in the Great Basin, a few settlements scattered hither and yon, and Indians clinging to life on barren reservations, the West was, for the most part, still empty.

How to fill it up?

First, it was a matter of establishing reliable communication and connections with its far-flung places. Barring a brief interruption while otherwise occupied with the Civil War, the government and private enterprise waged a continual and concerted effort to establish links. There were the trails, of course, for both goods and emigrants, with the Platte River Road, dividing into the Oregon, California, and Mormon trails, being the main highway. The south had the Santa Fe Trail, the Fort Smith-Santa Fe

"Western emigration makes men larger, riper, and more fraternal."

ALBERT RICHARDSON
NEW YORK TRIBUNE REPORTER, 1865

By 1869, and the completion of the transcontinental railroad in Promontory, Utah, a journey that had once taken many months by wagons or many weeks by stagecoaches could now be accomplished in just a few days by rail.

Trail, and the Upper and Lower roads across Texas to the Southern and Gila Trails. There were also the Bozeman Trail, Applegate Trail, El Camino Real, and the Old Spanish Trail. All played important roles in moving America west.

A network of cattle trails out of Texas, well-known for feeding cattle to the East via railheads in Kansas, also stocked ranches in New Mexico, Colorado, Utah, Wyoming, Nebraska, the Dakotas, and Montana.

Mail, express, and stage routes—the Butterfield Route through Texas, New Mexico, and Arizona; Chorpenning's "jackass mail" across the Great Basin; the Central Overland Trail; the short-lived Pony Express—established regular service between East and West.

The transcontinental telegraph linked up in Salt Lake City in 1861 and spread tentacles in every direction, creating the nineteenth-century version of the Internet.

Everything changed with the completion of the transcontinental railroad at Promontory, Utah, in 1869. Spur routes and trunk lines and connector routes soon stitched the West togeth-

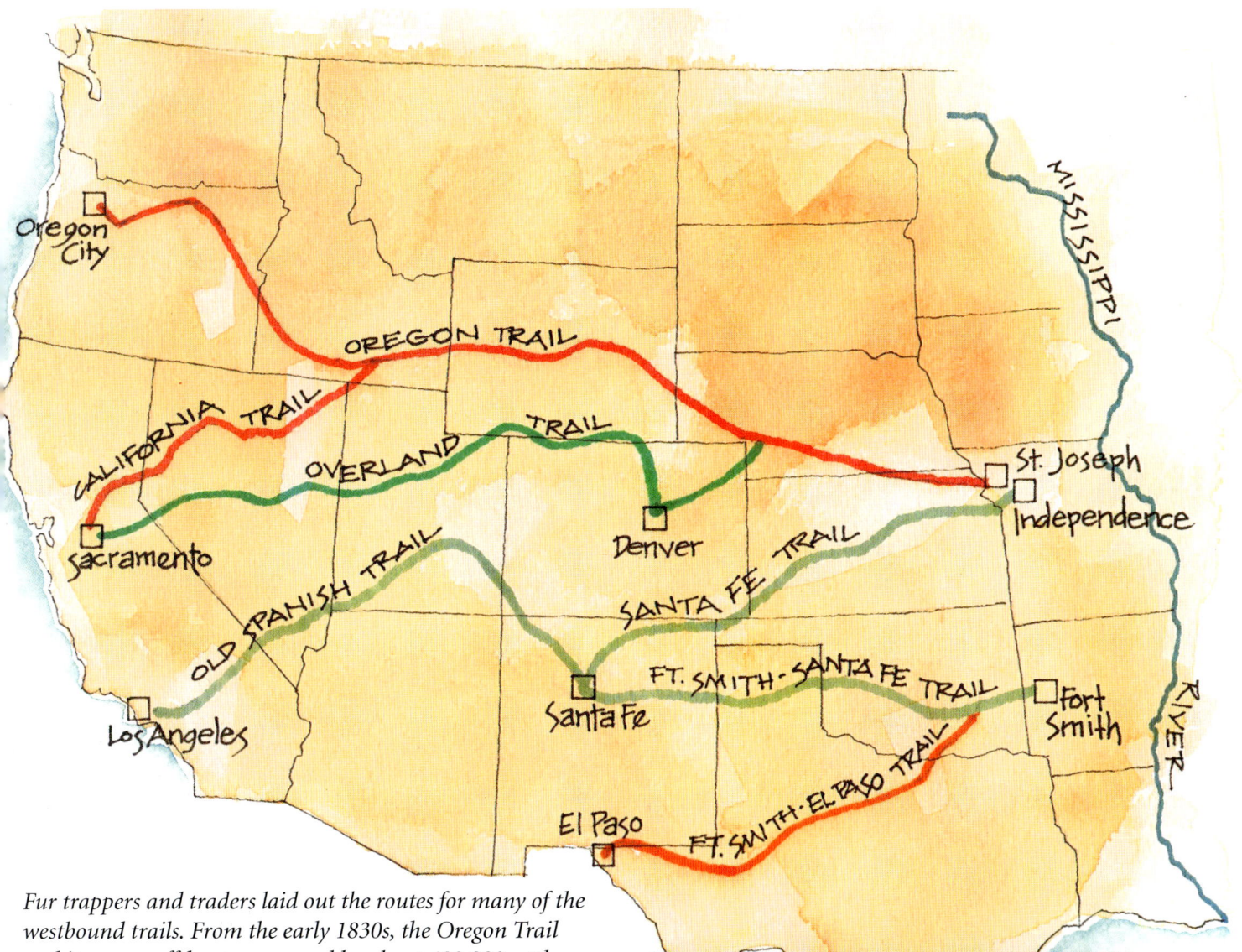

Fur trappers and traders laid out the routes for many of the westbound trails. From the early 1830s, the Oregon Trail and its many offshoots were used by about 400,000 settlers. Illustration © John Bardwell

er, and rapid movement of goods and people throughout the region and seamlessly to the East made all things possible. A journey that had once taken many months by wagons or many weeks by stagecoaches could now be accomplished in a few days by rail.

Real estate speculators, western states and territories, and the railroads themselves launched incessant marketing campaigns in the East and even in Europe urging people to "Go West" where they would find unlimited prospects, opportunities, and, most of all, land. A steady stream of settlers took the bait, and the population of the West grew. With the passage of the Homestead Act of 1862, this stream became a torrent.

The Homestead Act allowed anyone over age twenty-one to lay claim to 160 acres of land, live on and improve it for five years, and win the title. Well-intentioned though it was, the

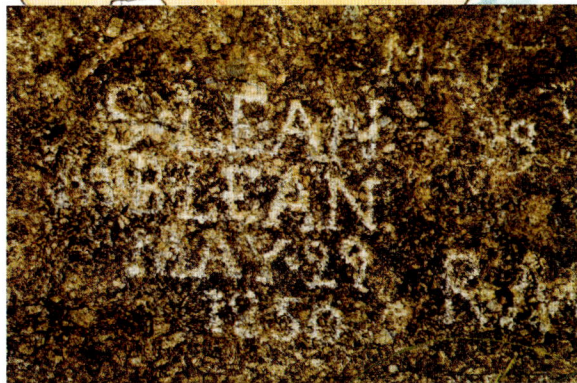

Historic inscriptions of California and Oregon Trail pioneers on the surface of Independence Rock, Wyoming.

"I wanted to be the first to view a country on which the eyes of a white man had never gazed and to follow the course of rivers that run through a new land."

JEDEDIAH SMITH
EXPLORER AND MOUNTAIN MAN, 1826-1827

The horned lizard is also called horned toad, horny toad or horned frog, but it is neither a toad nor a frog. This camouflaged lizard was found in Dublin Gulch in Death Valley, California.
© Larry Angier

Little Colorado River Gorge in northeast Arizona is known by the Navajo people as Little C. This river joins the mighty Colorado at the Navajo Indian Reservation and the Grand Canyon.
© Richard Menzies

Pioneer women had to be brave, tough and resilient. If they were lucky, they lived in a soddy, made from dirt, manure and grass—the only materials found on the Plains.

Between emigrants and freighters, jumping off places in the Midwest were often congested. Traffic thinned out on the Plains.

Woman and girl gathering buffalo chips to use as fuel for cooking in the 1800s.

"There is among western women a universal hopefulness and aspiration."

HJALMAR BOYESEN, 1889 EMIGRANT

Homestead Act was based on Eastern notions of landholding and soon proved unworkable in the West. By 1900, every acre of well-watered land where living was possible was taken. Fraud ran rampant, with false filings and consolidation of claims that tied up the water. The government's answer was to increase allowable acreage to 320 acres for dryland farming and 640 acres for livestock ranching. Even free, most of the land out West went wanting and stayed in the public domain.

When all was said and done, some four million settlers took up homesteads on 270 million acres in thirty states. Less than half of the claimants "proved up" and stuck to the land. Many who stayed to grow crops on the dry plains followed bad advice and futile farming practices, eventually turning much of the West into a dust bowl. Only by mining underground water is crop farming feasible in a land of little rain.

Ranchers could not raise enough cattle or sheep on 640 acres of rangeland to make a living, so the government eventually formalized and regulated public lands grazing to make livestock raising feasible for many western ranchers. It helped. The plains, mountains, and deserts of the West, when properly cared for, proved to be prime cattle country, adapted as they were to grazing by countless generations of buffalo.

But whether crops or cattle are being grown, out here it all comes down to water. Lacking rainfall, the West relies on mountain snowpack accumulated over the winter to get through the hot, dry summer. As explorer John Wesley Powell wrote: "When the summer sun comes, this snow melts and tumbles down the mountainsides in millions of cascades. A million cascade brooks unite to form a thousand torrent creeks; a thousand torrent creeks unite to form a half a hundred rivers beset with cataracts; half a hundred roaring rivers unite to form the Colorado, which rolls, a mad, turbid stream, into the Gulf of California." While Powell's lyrical description is of the Colorado River watershed, the same holds true, more or less, throughout the West. Water—or lack of it—remains the West's defining factor, and always will.

It's a definition that forces scattered population centers, with wide-open spaces in between. Get out of town out West, and you'll find miles and miles of little but miles and miles in every direction. At least that's what it seems like to the uninitiated. Those miles still, and always will, support a way of life unique to America. Cattle ranching, with its horseback cowboys riding the range tending cattle, symbolizes our nation to the rest of the world and gives us an identity, a culture, like no other.

Cowboying represents freedom and independence, individuality and cooperation, perseverance and competence, and just about any quality you care to attach to it. From the day-to-day reality of ranching to the mythologized popular culture it spawned, from the wide-open spaces to the communities that ranching supports—and that support ranching—the West grew up to become America. The nation embraced the qualities, values, and ideals of the West and they have come, perhaps more than anything else, to define our country. As Wallace Stegner, dean of western writers, said, "One cannot be pessimistic about the West. This is the native home of hope."

And so, the words "Go West" still have meaning.

Go West to the rolling grasslands of the Great Plains, to the sagebrush seas of the Great Basin and Snake River Plain.

Go West to the picturesque peaks of the Tetons, the Ruby Mountains, the Wasatch, the Sawtooths, the Rockies, the Bitterroots, the Black Hills, the Superstition Mountains, the Sierra.

Go West to the folded, wrinkled, and warped sandstone of the Colorado Plateau, the red-rock monuments of the Four Corners, the shifting sands of the Mojave.

Go West to the roiling waters of the Salmon River, the meandering flow of the Humboldt, the pristine drift of Henry's Fork, the wandering of the Rio Grande, the mighty Missouri, the Platte, the Arkansas.

Go West to the ruins of ancient civilizations, to ghost towns of days gone by, to communities that cling to little but courage and optimism, and to cities that crowd the limits of nature.

Go West to...well, to the West. ■

The Risk

The decision to Go West was an all-in bet. For most emigrants, it meant putting up everything they had in the way of earthly riches to outfit themselves for the trail and the life they envisioned on the far side of the plains.

It was anything but a sure bet. In fact, it was an outright gamble. Odds were that one of every ten people—men and women, young and old, rich and poor—who started the trip would never finish it. All faced a ten percent chance of dying on the journey.

The trail was fraught with dangers and difficulties. Death from disease was commonplace. Accidents, an everyday occurrence. Starvation took its toll. Indian attacks, more dangerous in myth than reality, required vigilance nevertheless. Over the

years, some 65,000 people died—enough to populate a good-sized western city even today. You could not walk the emigrant roads without stepping over countless graves, most unmarked and forgotten, as memorialized in the poem "Manifest Destiny":

Skeletons, like trusses, rafters, beams,
prop up this trail of ruined dreams
as parades of hopeful pilgrims tread
a road buttressed by bones of the dead.

The first challenge was simply finding the fortitude to put one foot in front of the other, day after day after day for miles and months on end. For, despite the movie version where happy families rode the wagons, most people walked every step of the way. Wagons were overloaded with supplies, and no one rode save those gravely ill or otherwise indisposed. Some hadn't the luxury of wagons at all. Recall the storied Mormon handcart companies. Many a forty-niner set out with nothing more than a wheelbarrow; others had only a rucksack and a dream.

Cholera was a cruel killer, filling many a grave and laying survivors low with pain and suffering. Martha Freel, an 1852 emigrant, wrote, "We have lost seven persons in a few short days, all died of cholera."

And accidents. Absolom Harden wrote in 1847 of an eight-year-old boy who tried to climb into a wagon and "fel from the tung. The wheals run over him and mashed his head and Kil him Ston dead he never moved." Others died from inad-

Winnemucca dunes,
Humboldt County, Nevada.
© Susan Summer Elliott

vertent gunshots, were trampled or gored by draft animals, drowned in stream crossings.

Some starved.

Some were massacred, including 120 or so innocent emigrants murdered by Mormons and a few Indians at Mountain Meadows in 1857. Most deaths at Indian hands occurred in the Great Basin and on the Snake River Plain as Shoshoni and Paiute bands sought retribution and revenge as the years of emigration wore on. But it wore on.

"Go West," they said. And go they did, by the tens of thousands. Suffering took its cut. Death got a share. For all and every one, it was a trip rife with risk. ■

Buffalo cow and calf.
© Diane McAllister

Buffalo graze in the shadow of the Tetons in western Wyoming. © Willie Felton

"The West! The mighty West! That land where the buffalo still roams and the wild savage dwells; where the broad rivers flow and the boundless prairie stretches away for thousands of miles; where the poor, professional young man, flying from the overcrowded East and the tyranny of a moneyed aristocracy, finds honor and wealth!"

JAMES S. BRISBIN, 1881

"When the summer sun comes, this snow melts and tumbles down the mountainsides in millions of cascades. A million cascade brooks unite to form a thousand torrent creeks; a thousand torrent creeks unite to form a half a hundred rivers beset with cataracts; half a hundred roaring rivers unite to form the Colorado, which rolls, a mad, turbid stream, into the Gulf of California."

JOHN WESLEY POWELL
SCIENTIST AND EXPLORER, 1869

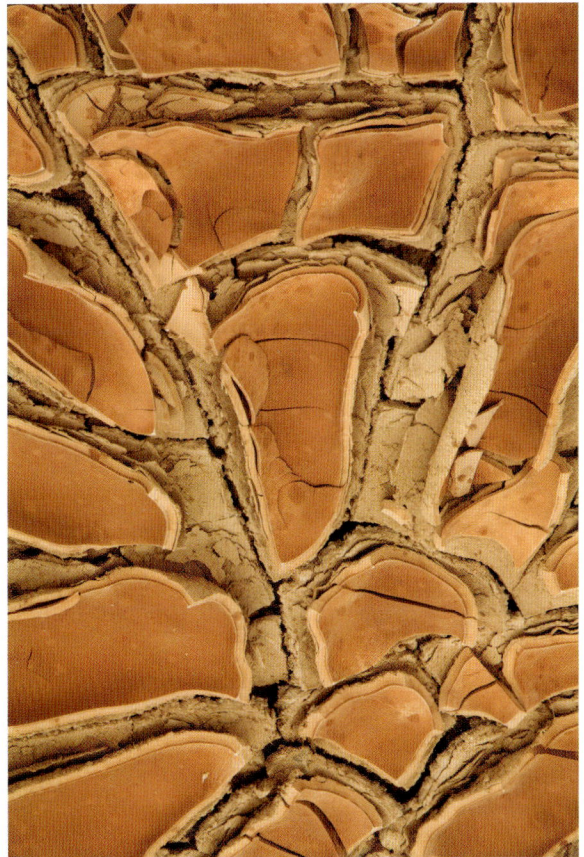

Drying, cracked mud at Sperry Wash in San Bernardino County, California. © Larry Angier

Flowing water from spring runoff in the upper north fork of the Mokelumne River near Calaveras Dome in Amador County, California. © Larry Angier

27

"One cannot be pessimistic about the West.
This is the native home of hope."

WALLACE STEGNER, AUTHOR, 1909-1993

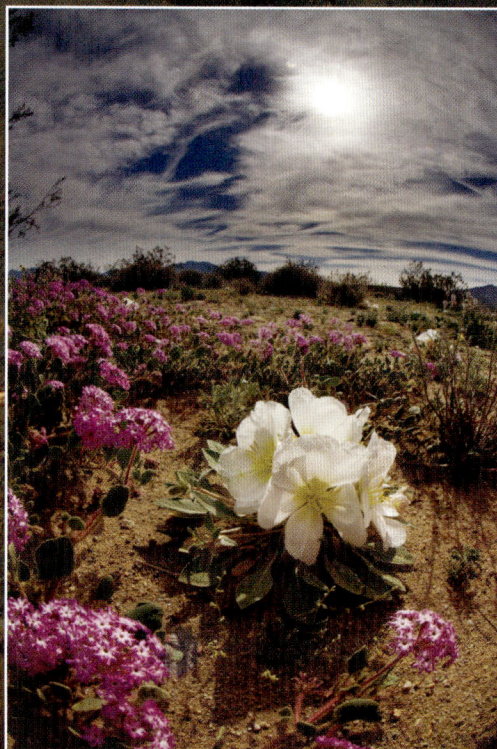

*Desert evening primrose
and sand verbena flowers,
springtime on Kelso Dunes
in California's Mojave
Desert. © Larry Angier*

*Dunes north of
Winnemucca, Nevada.
© Susan Summer Elliott*

"In the West, you take people at their word."

KEN SALAZAR, SECRETARY OF INTERIOR
FOR PRESIDENT OBAMA, BORN 1955

*View from the top of Summit Lake Mountain,
Humboldt County, Nevada. © Linda Dufurrena*

Coyote pups. Females bear from three to nine puppies a year. These wild canines are inspired and aggressive predators.
© Tammy L. Hoover

Long-eared owlet.
© Diane McAllister

Bighorn sheep horns can weigh up to thirty pounds, while their body weight averages 300 pounds.
This species originally crossed to North America over the Bering Land Bridge from Siberia.
These bighorn bucks were found in Big Smoky Valley in central Nevada. © Barry Glazier

"We were starting across a desert, seventy miles without water.
In two days we were to cross, thirty-five miles a day, fifteen
miles farther than our average distance. It was to
be two long and terrible drives for horses as worn and thin as
ours. Only a bit of grass, mowed and carried with us,
we had to feed them those two days. Out upon the lava beds
we rumbled, the hollow, echoing, metallic roar sounding as if
we were upon a great bridge. At daylight there lay
around us a gray and desolate waste."

PHILURA V. CLINKINBEARD, EMIGRANT, 1864,
AS RECOUNTED BY HER DAUGHTER ANNA DELL CLINKINBEARD

The Humboldt Sink
close to Lovelock Caves
on the Old California Trail.
© Linda Dufurrena

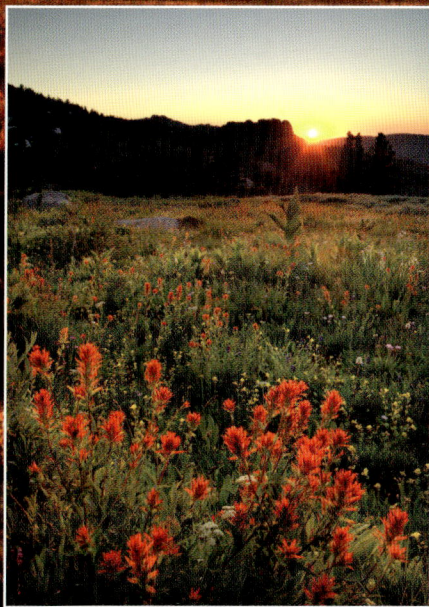

A field of wildflowers near Lake Winnemucca.
© Larry Angier

Dandelion at sunset.
© Larry Angier

Eagle River flows from the Rocky Mountains near Leadville and heads north through one of the old gold and silver mining territories of Colorado. It continues north and flows through the old mining town of Red Cliff, which was known for its gold rush in the late 1800s. © Klaus Girk

Free-roaming horses in the Pinenut Mountains near Virginia City, Nevada.
© Kevin Karl, www.kevinkarlphoto.com

*Mustang studs fight for
mares in Nevada's high,
dry desert valleys.
© Patricia Neely*

"It's a landscape that has to be seen to be believed. And as I say on occasion, it may have to be believed in order to be seen."

N. SCOTT MOMADAY, KIOWA-CHEROKEE WRITER, BORN 1934

Park Avenue
Arches National Park, Utah.
© Richard Menzies

Petroglyphs from Rochester site rock art panel in the San Rafael Swell in Utah. Some of the images instilled fear in the pioneers, others inspired hope. © Larry Angier

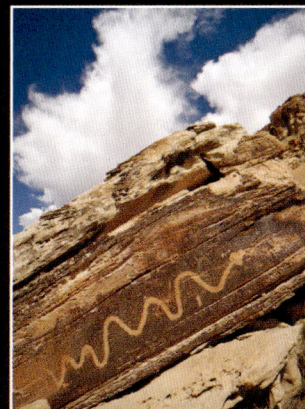

"The finest country in the world.
Women is all that is needed."

SETH SMITH, CALIFORNIA PIONEER BORN 1829

Saguaro cactus and clouds,
Arizona. © *Larry Angier*

Snow geese swarm by the gaggle to feed on gleanings in a plowed field. This is late afternoon at Tule Lake in Siskiyou County, California.
© Larry Angier

Mexican ground squirrel emerges from its burrow in Texas.
© Scott Linstead/Tom Stack & Associates

Nevada mule deer bucks.
© Tammy L. Hoover

"The West is color. Its colors are animal rather than vegetable, the colors of earth and sunlight and ripeness."

JESSAMYN WEST, WRITER, 1902-1984

Sunset over the receding ridges and
foothills of the Sierra Nevada from
Peddler Hill near Jackson, California.
© Larry Angier

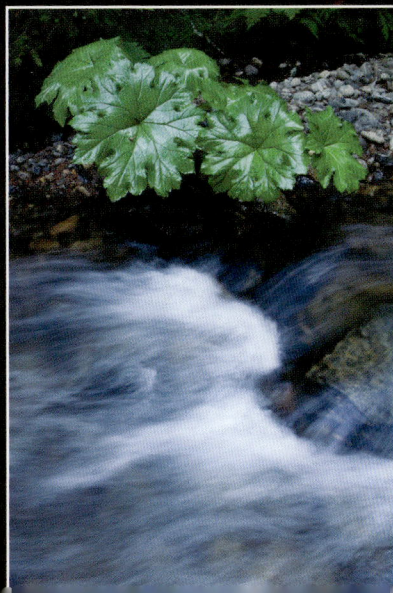

Indian rhubarb,
Sierra Nevada.
© *Larry Angier*

Osprey, common to the Rocky Mountains, can dive. It feeds mainly on fish, its feathers are water resistant, and its talons (two front, two back) hold tight to slippery prey. The female is larger than the male and can be twenty-two to twenty-five inches in length with a wing span up to seventy-two inches. Osprey can carry a two-pound fish and prefers to hunt over open water. © Klaus Girk

Black bear with a kokanee salmon, Taylor Creek, South Lake Tahoe, California. © Linda Hammond

Elk graze near the famous Salmon River in northern Idaho. A hatch of insects are backlit in the scene. © Larry Turner

Organ Pipe Cactus National Monument in Arizona, which adjoins Sonora, Mexico.
© *Larry Angier*

Long Canyon, Laguna Creek, now known as Navajo National Monument, Arizona. © Larry Angier

Valley of Fires in the malpais of the Tularosa Valley, New Mexico.
© *Larry Angier*

> "Do I regret coming?
> No, far from it. I would not go
> back for the world. I am
> contented and happy,
> notwithstanding I sometimes
> get very hungry and weary."

OREGON PIONEER WOMAN, 1891

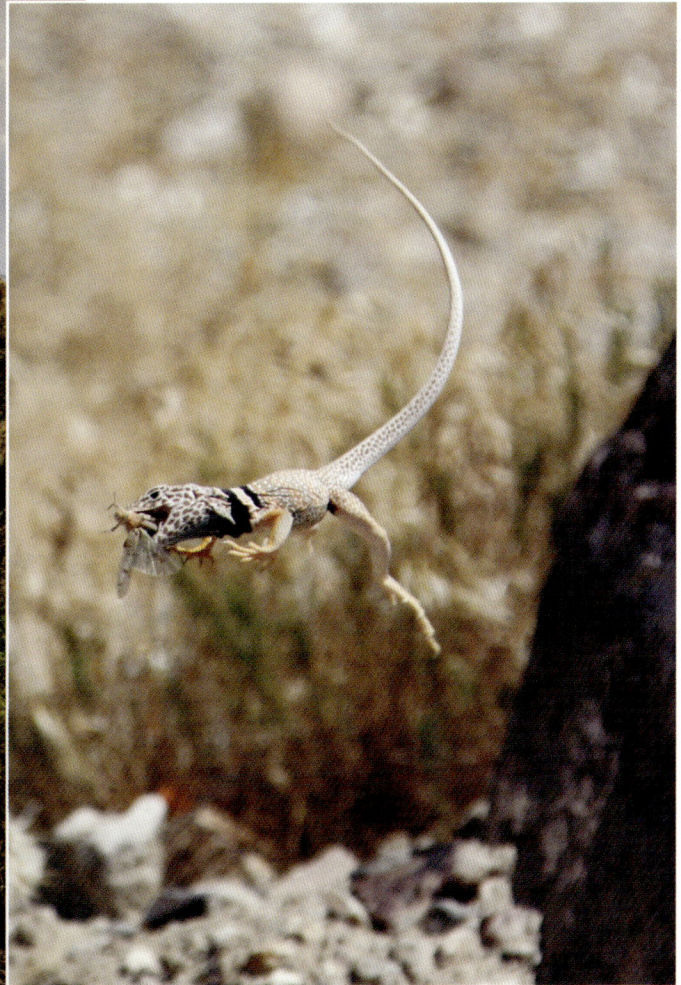

Lizard with lunch.
© Sheree Jensen

Milky Way over Lake Jackson in the Grand Tetons, Wyoming.
© Royce Bair, www.NightScapePhotos.com

Coyote foreplay.
© *Marsha Hiatt*

*Middle deer, possibly the matriarch,
is a rare silver color. This group is in the
Ruby Mountains in eastern Nevada.
© Mark Hayward*

"The West of the old times
with its strong characters,
its stern battles and
its tremendous stretches of
loneliness, can never
be blotted from my mind."

BUFFALO BILL, FRONTIERSMAN, 1846-1914

*Battling bighorn rams.
© Marion Dickinson*

*A huge area of rugged land west and south of Moab, Utah, consists of
canyons and plateaus carved by two mighty rivers—the Colorado and
the Green. This is the view from Boulder Mountain of what is now
known as Canyonlands National Park. © Richard Menzies*

Surviving the Risk. Earning the Reward.

Some who headed West abandoned hope and turned back along the trail before ever getting there. Others, having arrived, starved out or, overcome with disappointment, returned to the East. Many a homesteader abandoned an isolated claim. Loneliness sometimes resulted in insanity and suicides, particularly among women. Some hopeless men went out to chore one morning and simply walked away, leaving families to their own devices.

Still, despite the hardships, despite the suffering, despite the difficulty, they kept coming. Meldrum Crawford, an 1842 emigrant, wrote, "The westward surge was a human instinct, like the need to love or to taste spring and believe again that life is not a dead end after all." Said Jesse Quinn Thornton, an 1846 emigrant, "They agreed in the one general object—that of bettering their condition."

So most looked beyond the despair to see opportunity at every hand. In talking about the "Great American Desert" and the arid expanse of the Great Basin, forty-niner Jasper Hixson wrote, "There were millions of acres better than some of our older states, and tens of millions that would be called a paradise by those living in the north of Europe."

And some saw through the formidable barriers the western landscape presented to appreciate its beauty. "The Alps, so celebrated in history and by all travelers as admirers of mountain landscape, cannot, I am satisfied, present scenery more wild, more rugged, more grand, more romantic, and more enchantingly picturesque and beautiful than that which surrounds this lake, of which the lake itself composes a part," Edwin Bryant, an 1846 emigrant, wrote at Truckee Lake in the Sierra Nevada range.

For most, the possibilities were there, waiting to be realized. Waiting for people with the optimism, the attitude, the aptitude, to build communities, culture, a civilization in the West. One California emigrant, Seth Smith, thought he had the answer when he said the West was "The finest country in the world. Women is all that is needed."

*Summer evening lightning strikes the
Indian Benches on the Colorado Plateau,
San Juan County, Utah. © Larry Angier*

The Reward

Seth Smith was probably right when he opined that the West needed women. For, despite the many accomplishments of men, it was women who "settled" the West, who brought stability, purpose, and permanence. Their influence resulted in churches and schools, in cultural entertainments, in social life, in wholesome pleasures.

Women "stuck," against all odds. As Oregon pioneer Narcissa Whitman reminisced in 1891: "Do not think I regret coming. No, far from it. I would not go back for the world. I am contented and happy, notwithstanding I sometimes get very hungry and weary." What 1889 emigrant Hjalmar Boyesen observed may well have been, and may still be, true: "There is among western women a universal hopefulness and aspiration."

Not that all was sunshine and roses in the settlements. As "Pink S," a brothel keeper, wrote in an 1859 letter about growing Denver, "The Emigration is comeing in continually and our town is building almost like a 2d sanfrancisco. It already contains any amt. of Liquor and gambling saloons, and one or two H Hs or assignation houses are to be supplied from Mexico and St. Louis & Cincin…" Bon vivant Oscar Wilde included Leadville, Colorado, on his itinerary and there toured an underground mine. He said, "Having got into the heart of the mountain, I had supper, the first course being whisky, the second whisky, the third whisky."

Rough edges and all, men, too, to some extent, eventually settled in the West. Another outsider, Albert Richardson, a reporter for the New York Tribune, observed in 1865 that "western emigration makes men larger, riper, and more fraternal." Pioneer, miner, Indian agent, politician, and, finally, Montana rancher, Granville Stuart told how westerners would make workaday ranch life a "fraternal" occasion: "The horse herder in

Summer storm brews above grazing cattle near Otter Creek, Utah.
© Larry Angier

Evening on the prairie near Alamosa in southern Colorado. © Bruce Most

charge of the horse wranglers would lead off in the direction of the objective corral followed by the white-covered four-horse chuck wagons, and then troops of cowboys with their gay handkerchiefs, fine saddles, and silver mounted bridles and spurs" followed, all with an object to work up a companionable sweat in the dust and smoke and stink of a branding pen.

The picture Stuart paints is a familiar one to westerners, even today. Now, as then, community, companionship, and camaraderie coexist comfortably with fierce self-reliance, independence, and individuality.

And therein, perhaps, lies the real reward of the American impulse to "Go West." Westerners built, and maintain, a rich, diverse, ever-changing culture that clings to the best but readily embraces the better, no matter its source. Such people are the heart of the West.

But, still, it is the wide-open spaces, the mountains and valleys, the plateaus and plains, and all the rest of the rich, varied landscape of the West that is its soul.

If you dare doubt it, find out for yourself. Go West. ■

Good? Or evil? The invention of barbed wire, patented in 1874 and a cheap and effective fencing material, put an end to open range in the West and the associated range wars and battles between ranchers and farmers. But, in the process, it caused its share of conflict and killing. Fence crews and fence cutters alike died as the wire stretched its way across the West. The barbed barrier also prevented cattle from drifting before a blizzard and was blamed for many livestock deaths during severe winter storms in the 1880s.
© Scott Baxter

*Shawn Schacht throws a long loop to catch a flying calf at Dick and Linda Huntsbergers'
branding in Bridgeport Valley, California. The Huntsbergers run 400 pairs on high-country
summer pastures leased from the Hunewill Ranch, which was homesteaded in 1861.
© Gary Butler*

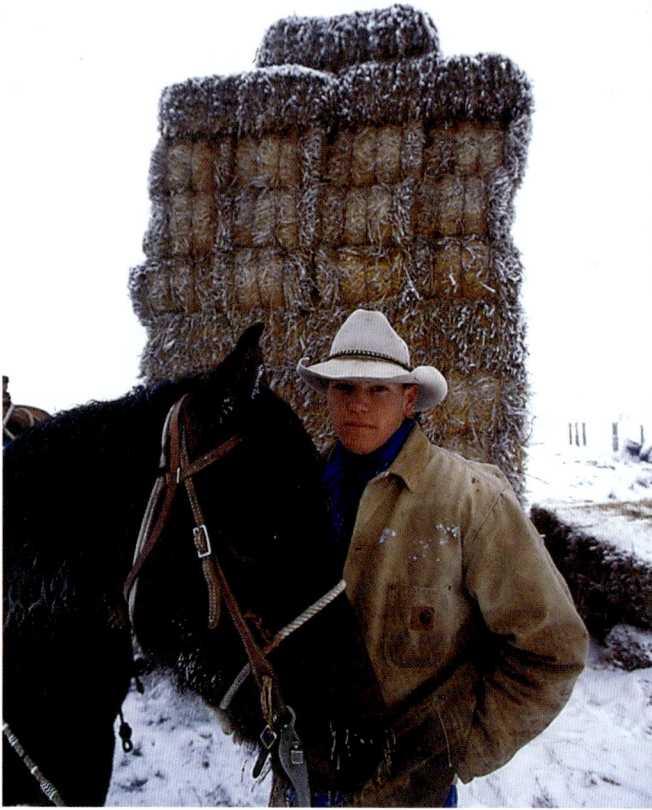

Cowboy Jack Armstrong takes a short break
from feeding winter hay in Malin, Oregon.
© Larry Turner

Brothers Bije, left, and Chip Lowe
regroup before sorting cattle on the
Nicholson Ranch in Kuna, Idaho.
When the cows and calves are moved
to the mountains in summer, a big
branding will be held over the
Fourth of July. It is also a weekend
celebrating friends and family.
© Andrea Scott

> "There's something special about an empty road going on and on and on to the horizon where the sun burns the world away into a dancing, shimmering heat haze that reflects the crystal blue sky, literally blurring the line between heaven and earth."
>
> DAVE GORMAN, BRITISH WRITER AND PRODUCER, 2008

Remnants of home sweet home, Unionville, Nevada. Sometimes, settlers could not overcome the risks. Only about half of those who took up homesteads in the West proved their claims, driven off the land by lack of water, hard winters, severe storms, accidents, death, and any number of other reasons. Some returned to more settled regions back East, others looked elsewhere in the West for land to claim, some took town jobs, became day workers on ranches, or turned their hand to any occupation that would allow them to survive in the harsh land they had come to love. © Susan Summer Elliott

Typical Great Basin ranch country. This is northeastern Nevada.
© Mark Hayward

Loving the work, rounding up goats in Smith Valley, Nevada. Chicken is a national champion border collie herding dog.
© Gary Butler

Rachael and Trixie are helping move cattle off BLM land in fall. They are heading to the home corrals at the Winnemucca Ranch in northern Nevada. The Dogskin Mountains are in the background.
© Debbie Bell

Brycen Martin has fun jumping
bales while his dad loads the feed
wagon in North Powder, Oregon.
© Kelly Martin

Vance Vesco fixes fence in the
wildflowers on Mount Tobin in
Pershing County, Nevada.
Jersey Valley is in the background.
Vance is maintaining the Bureau of
Land Management's allotment
fence on steep, rocky ground. It's all
manual labor. © Angela Vesco

"To me, homesteading is the solution of all poverty's problems, but I realize that temperament has much to do with success in any undertaking, and persons afraid of coyotes and work and loneliness had better let ranching alone."

ELINORE PRUITT STEWART, WYOMING HOMESTEADER, 1913

Buster Dufurrena is shipping lambs from the home corrals at Dufurrena Sheep & Cattle Company in Denio, Nevada. Buster, the son of a Basque sheepherder, prefers the sheep. "They get two incomes, for meat and wool, and they are easy to work." The detriment to running sheep on open country is too many predators—including coyote, mountain lion, bear and wolf—and the bands have little protection except for the sheepherders and their burros and dogs.
© Linda Dufurrena

A foreign crew work in an efficient mobile sheep shearing trailer near Worland, Wyoming. These pros can fleece a ewe in two minutes flat.
© Marion Dickinson

> "The children of ranchers know what their fathers do all day, because their fathers take them along. They teach them the tools of their trade and how to use them."
>
> CAROLYN DUFURRENA, FROM "FIFTY MILES FROM HOME," 2001

Hank and Zack Dufurrena after a late afternoon of branding in the corrals at the Dufurrena Ranch.
© Linda Dufurrena

*Sheep country in the Bilt Creek
Mountains north of Winnemucca,
Nevada. © Carolyn Fox*

Trailing cattle across the White River for shipping day on the Quarter Circle XL Ranch south of Belvidere, South Dakota.
© Jean Laughton

Chris and Diana Ellwood are ready to help out at the Badure Ranch south of Belvidere, South Dakota.
© Jean Laughton

Cow watches her calf get branded and she doesn't like it. John Elliott is applying the Circle H iron while his smoky wife Betsy Hunewill Elliott keeps the calf stretched out and still. Three generations of the family still work on the Hunewill Ranch in Smith Valley, Nevada, and Bridgeport, California. © Gary Butler

Jake Trindle and Ray Marxer of the Matador Cattle Company, Dillon, Montana, are trailing yearling heifers from their summer pasture on top of Blacktail Ridge. A big job, since they have to descend from about 9,000 feet to a 6,500-foot elevation, and cattle don't like going down steep grades. © Susan Marxer

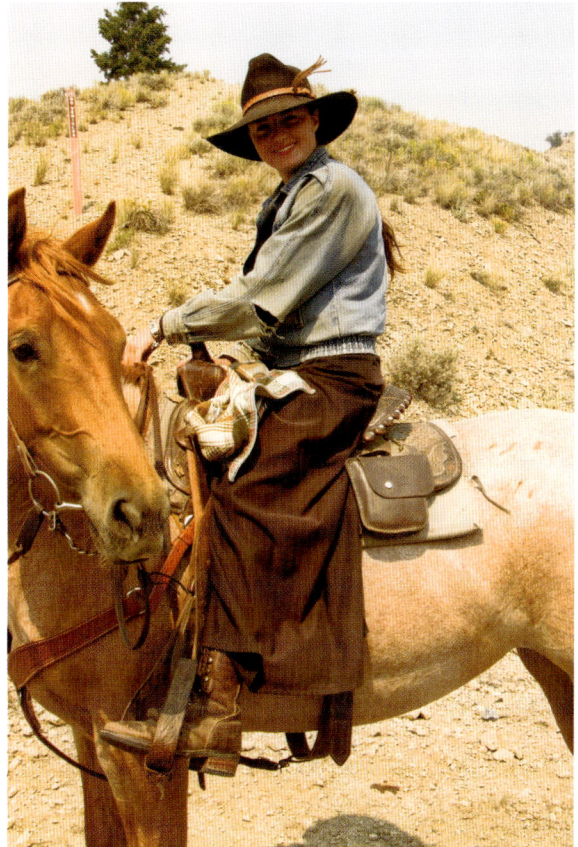

Carmen Lewis of the Lewis Ranch in Darlington is the quintessential cowgirl and is moving cows across country in central Idaho. She rides in gauchos everywhere she goes. Often the only girl out on the range, she sometimes finds herself in the midst of swearing cowboys but doesn't say a word; she just starts singing a hymn. Like magic, the swearing stops and the men simply smile.
© Linda Ellwein

Buckaroo Doug Groves works a young horse in the round corral at a northeastern Nevada cow outfit. © C.J. Hadley

Smoke Camp, Mays Land & Livestock. The herder's horse and dog wait for Gregorio, the Peruvian sheepherder, to emerge from his wagon and start the day. They will follow the sheep as they graze the hills near Jackknife Creek in Idaho. © Cindy Quigley

Manuel and dog watch over the sheep in Modoc County, California.
© Duane McGarva

Among a rancher's chores in the winter is the feeding of stock, especially during heavy snowstorms when grazing becomes challenging. This is the Hapgood Ranch near Lake City, California. © Larry Turner

Hailing from the Bluegrass state of Kentucky,
Roaring Springs Ranch buckaroo Matt Peak
takes a short break after a long day branding
in the high country of the Catlow Rim in
southeast Oregon. The ranch is based in
Frenchglen, Oregon. © Larry Turner

It's close to fall and cattle are driven from the Nevada range to the Estill Ranch in Eagleville, California. It is a three-day drive to bring the livestock off summer range. © Larry Turner

Clearing winter storm at Panther Creek, Eldorado National Forest, Amador County, California. © Larry Angier

Fort Klamath, Oregon, early morning on October 1. It's the first snow at the Agency Ranch and Wade Frutuozo, who works for the Holiday Ranch, gently drives cattle up the alley so that they can be weighed before shipping. © Deb Cockrell

Setting sun brings out the brilliance of the Ruby Mountains in eastern Nevada. © Susan Summer Elliott

Leslie Mortimer is a great mother, rancher and cowgirl. She is trailing cows back to the main ranch west of Casper, Wyoming.
© Carole C. Martinez

Future buckaroos, Nick and Damian.
© Linda Kennon Cassady

With his salt and red long mustache, buckaroo Charlie Smith of Boardman, Oregon, poses at Jordan Valley, Oregon's Annual Big Loop Rodeo. © Larry Turner

Bly, Oregon, River Springs Ranch manager Mike Eilmorini gets ready to slip into his "go-to-meetin' boots" after a morning of checking cattle in his work boots. © Larry Turner

A shepherd and his trusty dog watch the flock in the Warner Mountains of Northern California. It is evening, the day before shipping, so they need to keep the sheep close. © Duane McGarva

Mays Land & Livestock border collies keep the flock together. The ranch is based in Howe, Idaho. © Cindy Quigley

First steps.
© Diane McAllister

Minutes old and halfway there.
© Diane McAllister

Morning feeding of leppy lambs at Dufurrena Ranch, Denio, Nevada.
© Larry Angier

Rancher Jesse Hooker Davis (standing in back)
has lunch with his cowboys after spring roundup,
Sierra Bonita Ranch, Graham/Cochise County,
Arizona. The ranch was established in 1872.
© Scott Baxter

Cooper Mayfield, age two and a half, thinks
he's on top of the world riding trusty bridle
horse Tuck. This little buckaroo's rope rarely
leaves his hand and he would sleep with his
boots and spurs on if he could at the
Grindstone Ranch, Elk Creek, California.
© Chaley Harney

Jo Rodriquez of Corning, California, grew up on ranches throughout the West. Now retired, she enjoys summers in the Black Rock Desert where she works her opal mine, makes handmade jewelry, and swaps stories with visitors. © Rhonda Knox

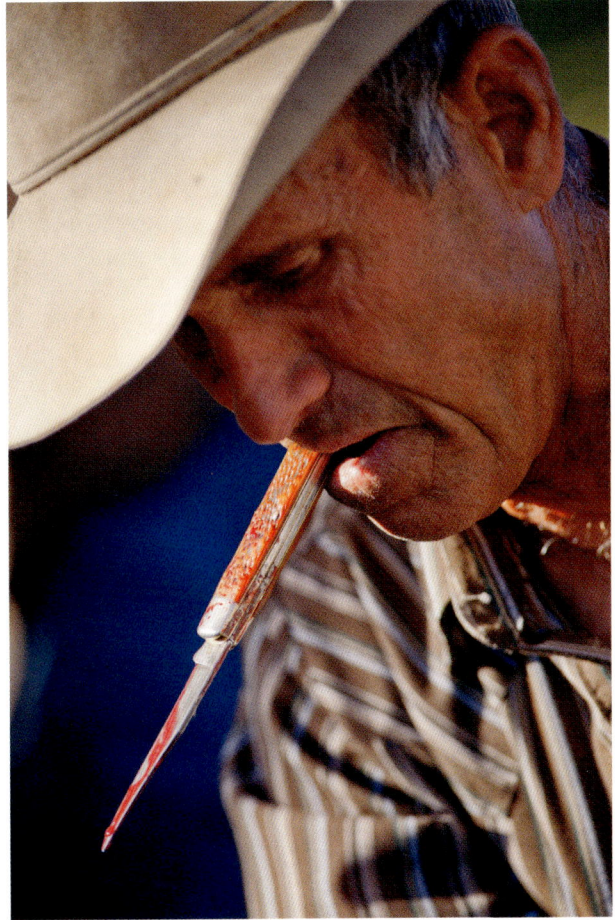

Steve Wooster, lifelong rancher from Calaveras County, is turning bull calves into steers during late-winter calf marking at the Dell'Orto Ranch in the Sierra foothills near Jackson, California. © Larry Angier

Gary Arballo, a longtime buckaroo at the famous ZX in Oregon, holds his friend's daughter, Erika Kerr, at the annual summer ZX Ranch Rodeo. © Larry Turner

Some ranchers and riders of Pass Creek Grazing Association near Mackay, Idaho, stop for a rare group shot at the Rams Horn Ranch corrals during a long day of riding and sorting. After a summer of shared grazing, cowboys and ranchers work together to ensure each ranch goes home with its own livestock. This annual event is a fun distraction from normal chores but it's bittersweet too—it's a reminder winter will soon again rear its ugly head in this high-altitude terrain. Left to right: Monte DelReal, Moj Broadie Jr., Trevor Arriaga, RJ Lundergreen, Travis Harrop, Mel Ellwein, Nolan Beard, Harry Crawford, and Harold Stein. © Linda Ellwein

Neighboring ranches near LaGrange, Wyoming, hold several brandings each spring, helping each other brand their cattle in groups of up to several hundred head. After cows and calves are gathered and brought to the corral, the calves are roped from horseback and "rassled" to the ground by hand to be branded, inoculated and marked. Traditional irons are heated in wood fires and cowboys have to be careful to use the right brand. Following the branding, the host ranch provides a feast for the workers and visitors. © Bruce Most

Surrounded by cowgirls at the Prather Ranch in Macdoel in Siskiyou County, California. From left: Madison Wilson, Elizabeth Estes, Sarah Estes, Trapper Cundall and Quiana Cundall. They were all playing around the barn and riding horses. © Mary Rickert

Little Whiskers with the mare band and other foals at the Dufurrena Sheep & Cattle Company north of Winnemucca, Nevada. © Linda Dufurrena

Dan and Cash Marxer of the Dragging Y Ranch in Horse Prairie, Montana, give high fives while trailing cattle to the high country. © Kari Walker

Branding boss Michael Goettle is helping grandparents, Earl and Glenna Stucky, sort cattle at the Stucky Ranch in Avon, Montana. © Trisha Goettle

Deven and Cathy Thompson with their ten-day-old son Bryce at the historic Roaring Springs Ranch in Catlow Valley, Oregon. Deven works as the cow boss and oversees five buckaroos, a herd of 7,000 mother cows, and a string of fifty horses. "I had Bryce in the saddle the day after he was born," says the twenty-six-year-old buckaroo. "And he was actually in the saddle the day of his birth. Cathy was roping and dragging calves at one of our brandings when her water broke and Bryce was born later that evening. Horseback from day one! Not many moms and dads can boast about that." © Larry Turner

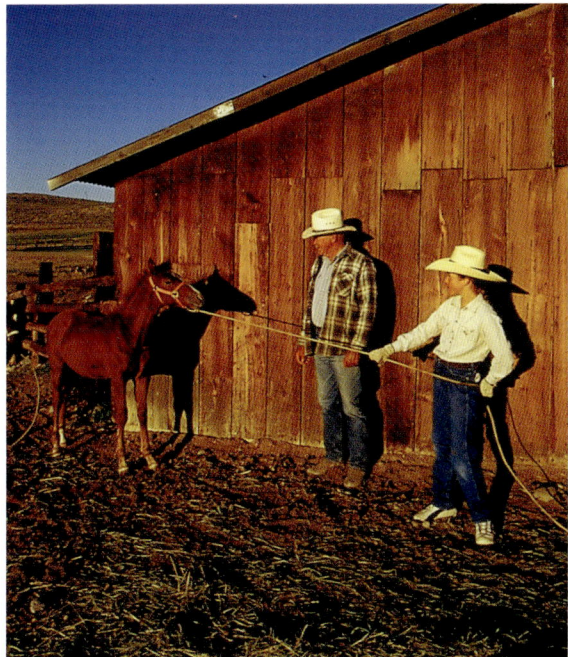

Lifelong rancher Ken Bentz instructs his granddaughter Erika Bentz on the technique of breaking a young colt in Drewsey, Oregon.
© Larry Turner

Yucca flowers, Culberson County, Texas. The yucca root and leaves can be used for inflammation and pain relief for arthritic and joint pain. Many herbalists and healers boil the yucca roots and drink it as a tea.
© *Larry Angier*

Moj Broadie Jr. of Broadie Ranches in Darlington, Idaho, heads out to gather cows and young calves on Pass Creek Summit, near Mackay, Idaho. The fresh spring feed and warming sun make the cows less than eager to move. Cows, horses, and cowboys make the steep climb to the summit by noon, but are only halfway to their high-mountain summer ground. © Linda Ellwein

Suzie Morton is caught by the camera as she unloads her horses after a long day of riding the range in Pass Creek, near Mackay, Idaho. Suzie is a true legend in central Idaho. There's not a rancher around who doesn't breathe a sigh of relief when she shows up.
© Linda Ellwein

This old sod-house post office was used until 1964 and is now a museum in Grassy Butte, North Dakota. Dee Fleck, longtime resident and former truck driver, poses in the lobby.
© Larry Angier

Jules Marchesseault
lives in Dillon, Montana,
with his wife Bonnie. His
father was also a rancher.
© Paul Mobley

Young roper Miguel Garcia stands
in the late light after an active day
of roping at a charro event near
Poteet, Texas. © Larry Turner

Rainbow with grazing horses and buckeye tree in Sutter Creek, Amador County, California. This was gold rush country. © Carolyn Fox

Curly checks the action at the Dufurrena Ranch near Denio, Nevada. © Linda Dufurrena

California cowboy catches this calf's back legs to drag it to the branding fire at the Hunewill Ranch in Bridgeport, California.
© Gary Butler

Riders from the south, Trevor Arriaga and RJ Lundergreen, working buckaroos for Three In One Ranch in Darlington, Idaho, take a break from sorting cows at the mouth of Pass Creek Canyon in central Idaho. Trevor and RJ are the best-dressed cowboys near Mackay, Idaho. They're some of the best help too. © Linda Ellwein

ZX Ranch buckaroos drive 3,000 cows to Poverty Basin outside Paisley, Oregon. The drive takes three days. © Larry Turner

The Schade Farm on the east side of the
Pine Forest Range near Denio, Nevada.
© *Linda Dufurrena*

One of the original homesteads on the A.J. and Alta Barker Ranch on Yellow Creek in Evanston, Wyoming. This was winter 2010, when snow was above normal. © Alta Barker

During a winter storm, feed rings for hay are moved by Todd McGiffin and his crew at the McGiffin Ranch in Fort Bidwell, California. Fresh hay is placed in the rings in wooden stalls and sometimes on the ground after being pulled by horse-drawn feed sleds into a nearby field. © Larry Turner

Indian nations. Spanish explorers. Catholic colonizers. Fur traders. Mountain men. Military mapmakers. Christian missionaries. Pioneer settlers. Mormon pilgrims. Forty-niners. Ranchers. Cowboys. Soldiers. Prospectors. Freighters. Homesteaders. Sheepherders. Loggers. Railroaders. Townsfolk.

All followed the admonition to "Go West." All left their marks on this land like no other. It took them all, and then some, to settle the West, to tame it as much as it can be tamed. The descendants of many of them are still here, debating, disagreeing, compromising, cooperating to make the West what it will become.

But, in the end, as it has always been, it will be the land that decides. And that is as it should be. Because, Horace Greeley aside, it was, and is, the land itself that called, and calls, us to "Go West."

Looking for cattle above
Spanish Flat Reservoir
near Doyle, California.
© Debbie Bell

Ridgetop north of Quinn River Ranch on the way to Kings River Valley in northern Nevada. It is a talus slope in volcanic rock ridges. The markings look like scratches from a giant cougar. © Linda Dufurrena

"The West is now closed."

Go West

Published by Range Conservation Foundation & RANGE magazine. © 2012

$32 U.S.